HOW TO MAKE AND USE
TALISMANS

A famous occult writer applies the traditional rules
in a modern manner, effectively dispelling the veils
of obscurity, and demonstrating how to construct
beautiful and effective talismans.

HOW TO MAKE AND USE TALISMANS

by

ISRAEL REGARDIE

THE AQUARIAN PRESS
Wellingborough, Northamptonshire

First published 1972
Third Impression 1977
This Edition, revised
and reset, 1981

British Library Cataloguing in Publication Data

Regardie, Israel
How to make and use talismans. – Revised ed.
1. Talismans
I. Title
133.4'4   GR600

ISBN 0-85030-209-9

Photoset by Specialised Offset Services Ltd., Liverpool
Printed in Great Britain by Lowe and Brydone,
Thetford, Norfolk
and bound by Weatherby Woolnough,
Wellingborough, Northamptonshire.

Contents

Dedication

This book was written for Sangreal Foundation (Dallas, Texas) at the suggestion of Mr Carr P. Collins, Jr. It is therefore with pleasure that I dedicate this work to
CARR P. COLLINS, Jr
and his gracious wife YYVONNE.

Biographical Note

Dr Francis Israel Regardie is one of the most distinguished and well-known occult writers of the twentieth century. His experience of practical and theoretical occultism stretches back over half a century.

Israel Regardie was born in London on 17 November 1907. In 1921 he left England to study in America, returning in 1928 to study under Aleister Crowley and to work as his private secretary. He was later secretary to the writer Thomas Burke.

In 1934 he joined the Order of the Golden Dawn, the most famous as well as the most important occult society to have emerged from the nineteenth-century occult revival. The Golden Dawn was formed in 1887 by three members of the Rosicrucian Society in England. René Guénon, in *Le Théosophisme* (1921), described the Golden Dawn as 'a society of occultists studying the highest practical magic, somewhat akin to Rosicrucianism'. Amongst the Order's members were S.L. MacGregor Mathers, A.E. Waite, W.B. Yeats, Arthur Machen, Charles Williams, and of course Aleister Crowley.

Israel Regardie took it upon himself to collect and edit the rituals of the Golden Dawn, which were first published in four volumes 1937–40. For this he was criticized by those who felt that the occult teachings of the Order should have remained well beyond the gaze of the merely curious. In the Introduction to a recent edition of *The Golden Dawn* Dr Regardie recalled the admonitions of J. Langford Garstin, a member of the Order, who chided him severely for publishing their secret teachings, asking him in the future never again to refer to the Golden Dawn by name. Crowley, too, wrote one of his last letters to Dr Regardie before their estrangement to state two things:

> First, in connection with my statement that one of the officiating officers had hurried through an initiatory ritual as though reading a batch of grocery bills – he remarked that I should have rudely told him to go to Jericho, or words to that effect. And secondly, relative to the material itself, he roundly scolded me, stating I had absolutely no right whatsoever to have published this material and to have broken my sacred obligation to secrecy.

But no student of twentieth-century occultism can regret that Dr Regardie felt compelled to make the Golden Dawn's teachings known beyond the confines of the Order. *The Golden Dawn* is his *magnum opus*, a fitting monument to a unique and influential society and to one of this century's greatest apologists for the aspirations it sought to enshrine.

Dr Regardie has also written on many aspects of Magic: his *Tree of Life* is now generally acknowledged to be one of the best books on the subject ever written. He has written extensively on the Qabalah, mysticism and meditation and is also the author of a penetrating biographical study of Crowley – *The Eye in the Triangle*. His principal essays on Magic, the Qabalah, Numerology, Meditation and Healing have recently been collected as *The Foundations of Practical Magic* (The Aquarian Press, 1979).

As well as his practical and theoretical experience of occult techniques, Dr Regardie brings to his work a solid grounding in other related disciplines. He was trained in Freudian, Jungian and Reichian methods, studied psychoanalysis with Dr E. Clegg and Dr J.L. Bendit, and later studied psychotherapy with Dr Nandor Fodor. He has taught psychiatry at the Los Angeles College of Chiropractic and his writings have appeared in the *Psychiatric Quarterly* and *The American Journal of Psychotherapy*. He lectures widely in the United States, where he now lives, or relaxation techniques, psychotherapy, magic and mysticism.

M.A.C.

1.

Origin of Talismans

A talisman is any object, sacred or profane, with or without appropriate inscriptions of symbols, uncharged or consecrated by means of appropriate ritual magic or meditation. Amongst other things it exerts an auto-suggestive effect on the wearer. It is made to serve a specific end, to bring good fortune in some area of life, or to achieve some specifically named goal.

An amulet is in effect no different, save that as a charm it is supposed to be worn for protection against disease, sickness, ill-fortune, or witchcraft.

For the purpose of this manual, the word talisman will be the preferred term. In passing, it should be emphasized that I have no fundamental objection to the theory of suggestion so long as it is clearly understood that suggestion cannot implant in or evoke from the psyche what is not already there. Suggestion is evocative only of those psycho-spiritual factors that are innate.

Golden Dawn Definition
According to the Golden Dawn's somewhat larger frame of reference, a talisman 'is a magical figure charged with the Force which it is intended to represent. In the construction of

a Talisman, care should be taken to make it, as far as is possible, so to represent the universal Forces that it should be in exact harmony with those you wish to attract, and the more exact the symbolism, the more easy it is to attract the Force – other things coinciding, such as consecration at the right time, etc.'

In the West, talismans are traditionally inscribed with Hebrew words and sentences – demonstrating that the Qabalah is a major influence – or sometimes with Latin and Greek.

No student should attempt to make any talisman without having familiarized himself in large measure with the occult and philosophical principles underlying the Qabalah. Then he will know something of the Qabalistic Tree of Life and its philosophy. This will render unnecessary any protracted examination of those principles in this time and place.

Some of the books mentioned in the bibliography provide sigils and pantacles on which are inscribed complex symbols and names whose Graeco-Hebrew and Latin origins are almost impossible to trace. (Incidentally, the word Sigil merely means 'signature'. So that the sigil of an Archangel is really the symbolic signature of that Being. These sigils were originally extracted from the traditional Kameas or magical squares, which will be described in due course.) For our present purpose, these will have to be ignored, since what is required beyond all other things is a system which is clear, sensible and workable.

Dynamic Purpose

Symbols of a wide variety from almost every conceivable source are employed to provide character and to give specificity to the dynamic purpose for which the talisman has been constructed. Planetary and zodiacal symbols are most common.

In addition, symbols and designs have been freely developed from the basic sixteen geomantic symbols whose origin is lost in the dimness of time past. These sixteen symbols, though attributed to the twelve signs and seven planets, may still be further reduced to the four elements, as indicated on the chart below.

Geomantic Symbols

Symbol Emblem

Element: △   ▽   ▽   △

Puer ♈	Via ♋	Amissio ♉	Albus ♊
Fortuna Minor ♌	Populus ♋	Conjunctio ♍	Puella ♎
Fortuna Major ♌	Rubeus ♏	Carcer ♑	Tristitia ♒
Acquisitio ♐	Laetitia ♓	Caput Draconis ☊	Cauda Draconis ☋

Only a little imagination is then required to transform the conventional symbol into a variety of shapes and forms, emblems, etc., which carry the geomantic meaning into activity.

From these latter alone, it is possible to construct a beautiful and effective talisman, without any supplemental aid. For example, the following is an example of a talisman using exclusively geomantic symbols that I made many years ago. It still strikes me as good design.

Obverse   *Reverse*

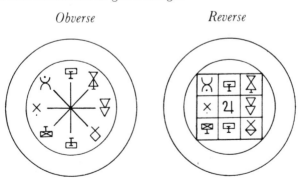

The basis of most talismans of old time were predicated either on the twelve signs of the zodiac or upon the seven planets known at that time. In other words, most subjects in which one could be interested were classified under one or other of these two sets of symbols. In the last resort, however, since the planets were said to rule the twelve zodiacal signs, the planets became the more prominent categories into which talismanic purposes could be divided. Classical examples of this seven-fold division of talismans may be found in *The Greater Key of King Solomon*, from which I quote as follows:

'*In the Days and Hours of Saturn*, thou canst perform experiments ... to cause good or ill success to business, possessions, goods, seeds, fruits and similar things, in order to acquire learning; to bring destruction and give death, and to sow hatred and discord.

'*The Days and Hours of Jupiter* are proper for obtaining honours, acquiring riches; contracting friendships, preserving health; and arriving at all that thou canst desire.

'*In the Days and Hours of Mars* thou canst make experiments regarding War; to arrive at military honour; to acquire courage; to overthrow enemies; and further to cause ruin, slaughter, cruelty, discord; to wound and to give death.

'*The Days and Hours of the Sun* are very good for perfecting experiments regarding temporal wealth, hope, gain, fortune, divination, the favour of princes, to dissolve hostile feeling, and to make friends.

'*The Days and Hours of Venus* are good for forming friendships; for kindness and love; for joyous and pleasant undertakings, and for travelling.

'*The Days and Hours of Mercury* are good to operate for eloquence and intelligence; promptitude in business; science and divination; wonders; apparitions; and answers regarding the future. Thou canst also operate under this Planet for thefts; writings; deceit; and merchandise.

'*The Days and Hours of the Moon* are good for embassies; voyages; envoys; messages; navigation; reconciliation; love, and the acquisition of merchandise by water.'

For example, should I crave honours and prestige, then Jupiter would be the planet ruling such matters, and the talisman would need to be constructed around the use of whatever symbols of Jupiter I could gather. Or, if I needed strength and aggressiveness in order to apply for a new, higher-paid position, or courage to beat a political opponent, then Mars would be the talismanic planet, and the symbols to be gathered should be martial. Should I want the love of a beautiful woman, then Venus becomes the presiding influence. And so on.

Personally Manufactured Talismans

An important consideration that needs emphasis is that the student's own personally manufactured talismans, while perhaps not as beautiful or as traditionally accurate as those given in some of the aforementioned texts, will nonetheless be more meaningful and effective for him. His very attempt to gather symbols and to draw them will, of itself, invest the talisman with energy and force that will tend to bring about the results desired.

One major injunction in *The Greater Key of King Solomon* is worthy of note here:

> 'I command thee, my Son, to carefully engrave in thy memory all that I say unto thee, in order that it may never leave thee. If thou dost not intend to use for a good purpose the secrets which I here teach thee, I command thee rather to cast this Testament into the fire, than to abuse the power thou wilt have of constraining the Spirits, for I warn thee that the beneficent Angels, wearied and fatigued by thine illicit demands, would to thy sorrow execute the commands of God, as well as to that of all such who, with evil intent, would abuse those secrets which He hath given and revealed unto me ...'

The traditional magical squares and sigils and hierarchical names have come down to us through the Abbot Trithemius, Pietro d'Abano, and Henry Cornelius Agrippa, derived from much earlier but unknown sources.

For the most part, these have been reprinted in *The Magus* by Barrett, were appropriated by the Hermetic Order of the Golden Dawn in the last century, and were once more reprinted by me when compiling the material for the fourth volume of *The Golden Dawn*. I would like to suggest that the interested student study this system at the very least, so that he will come to understand the classical basis of the method.

Magic Squares

The magic squares of the planets are an important part of the science of talismanic structure. To each planet belongs, first, the number of the *Sephirah* to which it corresponds; and secondarily, the other numbers which are the sum of the various horizontal and vertical rows on the square.

For example, Saturn is a planetary symbol of *Binah,* the third *Sephirah* on the Qabalistic Tree of Life. Thus the Square of Saturn has three compartments each way, and in each sub-division is a number of its square − 3 x 3 = 9, so that all numbers from one to nine are used and arranged so that the columns add up to 15 each way, and the three columns together total 45.

KAMEA OF SATURN

4	9	2
3	5	7
8	1	6

The Square of Jupiter, the planet attributed to the fourth *Sephirah* of *Chesed,* has sides of four divisions, or 4 x 4, resulting in 16 individual units, each line adding up to 34, of which the grand total is 136.

KAMEA OF JUPITER

4	14	15	1
9	7	6	12
5	11	10	8
16	2	3	13

Here is an example of the Square of Mars representing the fifth *Sephirah* of *Geburah*. Each side has 5 units for a total of 25 squares, with each line both sideways and up and down counting 65, the total being 325.

11	24	7	20	3	65
4	12	25	8	16	65
17	5	13	21	9	65
10	18	1	14	22	65
23	6	19	2	15	+65

65   +65   +65   +65   +65   =325

Similarly the four several numbers of the Sun are 6, 36, 111, and 666. The planet Venus equals 7, 49, 175, and 1225. The planet Mercury is represented by the numbers 8, 64, 260, and 2080. The Moon or Luna has the numbers 9, 81, 369, and 3321.

KAMEA OF SOL

6	32	3	34	35	1
7	11	27	28	8	30
19	14	16	15	23	24
18	20	22	21	17	13
25	29	10	9	26	12
36	5	33	4	2	31

22	47	16	41	10	35	4
5	23	43	17	42	11	29
30	6	24	49	18	36	12
13	31	7	25	43	19	37
38	14	32	1	26	44	20
21	39	8	33	2	27	45
46	15	40	9	34	3	28

KAMEA OF VENUS

8	58	59	5	4	62	63	1
49	15	14	52	53	11	10	56
41	23	22	44	45	19	18	48
32	34	35	29	28	38	39	25
40	26	27	37	36	30	31	33
17	47	46	20	21	43	42	24
9	55	54	12	13	51	50	16
64	2	3	61	60	6	7	57

KAMEA OF MERCURY

37	78	29	70	21	62	13	54	5
6	38	79	30	71	22	63	14	46
47	7	39	80	31	72	23	55	15
16	48	8	40	81	32	64	24	56
57	17	49	9	41	73	33	65	25
26	58	18	50	1	42	74	34	66
67	27	59	10	51	2	43	75	35
36	68	19	60	11	52	3	44	76
77	28	69	20	61	12	53	4	45

KAMEA OF LUNA

Each number total then becomes a name as, for example, in the case of Mercury, which represents the eighth *Sephirah* of *Hod*. Here the number 64 is DIN, a name meaning Justice, or its variation DNI, Doni. Its next number 260 is Tiriel, TIRIAL, the name of the Intelligence of this *Sephirah*, while 2080 is Taphthartharath, TPTRTRT, representing the Spirit of Mercury. In each one of these examples, sigils would be traced on the appropriate square by following the course of the numbers.

Basic to the use of the magic Squares is a method of permutation of Hebrew letters and numbers called 'The Qabalah of Nine Chambers'. It is produced by the interception of two horizontal and two vertical lines, forming nine squares, as follows:

THE QABALAH OF NINE CHAMBERS

Shin	Lamed	Gimel	Resh	Kaph	Beth	Qoph	Yod	Aleph
ש	ל	ג	ר	כ	ב	ק	י	א
300	30	3	200	20	2	100	10	1
Final Mem	Samekh	Vau	Final Kaph	Nun	Heh	Tau	Mem	Daleth
ם	ס	ו	ך	נ	ה	ת	מ	ד
600	60	6	500	50	5	400	40	4
Final Tzaddi	Tzaddi	Teth	Final Peh	Peh	Cheth	Final Nun	Ayin	Zain
ץ	צ	ט	ף	פ	ח	ן	ע	ז
900	90	9	800	80	8	700	70	7

This arrangement is called *Aiq Beker*. Reading from right to left we have *Aleph* = 1, *Yod* = 10, *Qoph* = 100. In the second chamber are *Beth* = 2, *Caph* = 20, and *Resh* = 200. Thus *Aiq Bkr*.

This arrangement of *Aiq Beker* is considered important in the formation of Sigils or Symbols from the names of the planetary Spirits. It is first necessary to reduce those letters and their numbers to tens or units by means of the above. For example, in the case of *Zazel*, the Spirit of Saturn, the letters are *Zayin* = 7, *Aleph* = 1, *Zayin* = 7, and *Lamed* = 30. The only letter which requires reduction in this instance will be Lamed which reduces to 3. The next step is to trace a continuous line on the magical square of Saturn. Thus in the name *Zazel*, the line will begin with the number 7, follow to 1, return to 7 again, and then end at 3. A little circle should be placed on the first letter of the Sigil to show where the name begins.

Classical Procedure

To illustrate one classical procedure, we might for example extract from the Mars square the Sigil of the intelligence *Bartzabel*. In Hebrew, this name is spelled:

Beth	Resh	Tzaddi	Beth	Aleph	Lamed
2	200	90	2	1	30

Three letters – *Resh*, *Tzaddi* and *Lamed* – will have to be reduced by *Aiq Beker*, so that their zeros will have been eliminated. Then, from the remaining numbers – 2, 2, 9, 2, 1 and 3 – we can trace the following sigil:

11	24	7	20	3
4	12	25	8	16
17	5	13	21	9
10	18	1	14	22
23	6	19	20	15

Sigil of Bartzabel superimposed on Mars Kamea

Another more prosaic example of tracing sigils from the magical squares can be demonstrated by taking my first name ISRAEL, and converting it into Hebrew, thus:

Yod	Shin	Resh	Aleph	Lamed
10	300	200	1	30

For the purpose of demonstration only, let us assume that we want to trace it on the magical square of the Sun.

6	32	3	34	35	1
7	11	27	28	8	30
19	14	16	15	23	24
18	20	22	21	17	13
25	29	10	9	26	12
36	5	33	4	2	31

Sigil of Israel superimposed on the Solar Kamea

Only *Shin* and *Resh* will have to be reduced by *Aiq Beker*, and they can be brought down to 30 and 20. So that, finally, the numbers we will use on the Square for the Sigil are: 10, 30, 20, 1 and 30.

To demonstrate this process further, mainly to illustrate the simplicity of sigils and magical designs that may be educed from the several kameas, consider the name Carr. In Hebrew we would spell it thus:

| *Caph* | *Aleph* | *Resh* | *Resh* |
| 20 | 1 | 200 | 200 |

The spelling of this name can then be applied to each planetary kamea, from which we would obtain a different sigil in varying planetary media. For example, to make a Saturnine sigil, we would have to reduce the letters by *Aiq Beker* to: 2, 1, 2, and 2. Its sigil would appear thus:

4	9	2
3	5	7
8	1	6

On the Jupiter kamea, which is four square, this is how the sigil would look:

4	14	15	1
9	7	6	12
5	11	10	8
16	2	3	13

At first sight it merely looks like the opposite form of the preceding Saturn sigil, which seems logical enough since Saturn is binding and Jupiter is opposite, expansive.

Consider the name on the Mars square. The process of reduction now operates differently. The *Resh*, 200, in this case has to reduce to 20, instead of to 2. This makes the Sigil turn out like this:

11	24	7	20	3
4	12	25	8	16
17	5	13	21	9
10	18	1	14	22
23	6	19	2	15

Most of the Sigils of this name, traced on other of the Kameas, will also prove very much alike, so there is little point proceeding further.

The critical student may, at this point, exclaim that Carr is a not frequently encountered name, so that the demonstration should proceed with more common names. For example, John, to be rendered in Hebrew, is *Yochanon*:

Yod	*Vau*	*Cheth*	*Nun*	*Nun*	*(final)*
10	6	8	50		700

In the event that the Solar Kamea is employed, both *Nuns* need to be reduced by *Aiq Beker* to 5 and 7. The Sigil superimposed on the Solar Kamea will appear thus:

6	32	3	34	35	1
7	11	27	28	8	30
19	14	16	15	23	24
18	20	22	21	17	13
25	29	10	9	26	12
36	5	33	4	2	31

Change in Numerical Value

This set of interesting but different designs demonstrates the enormous change in the numerical value of the name in the shift from one planetary influence to another. It represents the name first operating as one set of waves or frequencies and then as another, sliding as it were on a wide band of frequencies. Which frequency or kamea one may decide to use depends entirely on what function one wishes to stress. Here is where some slight understanding is required of the basic meanings of the planets in traditional astrology.

Incidentally, it makes little difference to this scheme whether one uses the traditional Hebrew system of gematria or numerology, or the more modern so-called Pythagorean numerology. The only criterion is consistency.

If one uses either of these two systems, it is essential to use it exclusively in any one operation. There is no reason at all why one should not be able to switch from one system to another. Just be consistent – and know what you are doing.

Evaluation in Western Numerology

In the Western system of numerology, the letters have this evaluation:

1	2	3	4	5	6	7	8	9
A	B	C	D	E	F	G	H	I
J	K*	L	M	N	O	P	Q	R
S	T	U	V*	W	X	Y	Z	

(I have placed an asterisk by the side of K and V, because they are considered as Master numbers, and should not be reduced if at all possible.)

Previously I used the name JOHN, transliterating it into Hebrew. This time, let us retain the English letters and name, using the above Western or Pythagorean system.

J	O	H	N
1	6	8	5

Solely for the purpose of illustration, let us trace this name JOHN on the Kamea of the Moon, which gives this Sigil:

37	78	29	70	21	62	13	54	5
6	38	70	30	71	22	63	14	46
47	7	39	80	31	72	23	55	15
16	48	8	40	81	32	64	24	56
57	17	49	9	41	73	33	65	25
26	58	18	50	1	42	74	34	66
67	27	59	10	51	2	43	75	35
36	68	19	60	11	52	3	44	76
77	28	69	20	61	12	53	4	45

To give another example, let me take the name of a friend VINCENT:

V	I	N	C	E	N	T
4	9	5	3	5	5	2

(Ordinarily in Western numerology, the vowels are separated from the consonants, but for the purpose of Sigil-making, we will not follow this custom.)

Now suppose Vincent wanted to stress success in his life by making a Sigil of his name on the Jupiter kamea, thereby linking himself with the expansive forces of Jupiter the Bestower, the sigil superimposed on the Jupiter kamea would appear thus:

4	14	15	1
9	7	6	12
5	11	10	8
16	2	3	13

Or the Sigil could be derived from the Solar kamea in order to establish a link between Vincent and the Source of Life and Light and success:

6	32	3	34	35	1
7	11	27	28	8	30
19	14	16	15	23	24
18	20	22	21	17	13
25	29	10	9	26	12
36	5	33	4	2	31

These several examples should suffice to demonstrate how both the Qabalistic and the Pythagorean systems of numbers may be used equally to good advantage in the formulation of Sigils from the traditional magical squares.

2.

How to Overcome
Unfavourable Aspects

Let us deal with another related phase of this topic. Suppose that you have had your horoscope erected by a competent astrologer, and the delineation indicates that too many planets are in Airy signs (Gemini, Libra, and Aquarius). If they are badly aspected, these planets *could* render the native rather flighty, relatively unstable, and impractical. In order to compensate for this, a talisman could be prepared which would balance out the unfavourable chart aspects. A Saturn talisman could, in these circumstances, be most useful.

Saturn Represents Balance
Saturn is not merely the grim reaper, the tester, the burden of life to be carried patiently on the shoulders. It also represents balance, equilibrium, and stability. It is the third *Sephirah* on the Tree of Life, *Binah*, the symbol of which is the triangle, the basic geometric figure representing harmony and order.

'The Mind of the Father said "Into Three", and immediately all things were so divided.' So stated the Chaldean Oracles. Then there is the cardinal tenet of the

Golden Dawn: 'There are always two contending forces, and a third which eternally reconciles them.'

Thus, logically, a Saturn talisman would be a superb characterological corrective to an overbalanced natal chart which stresses airy signs too much.

The first step would be to collect all the symbols of Saturn that would be available. The astrological symbol, the geomantic and geometric symbols, the Hebrew letter, the appropriate divine names from the appropriate *Sephirah* on the Tree of Life, etc. Having collected them, think of some phrase, scriptural or otherwise, which correctly summates the idea involved – stability. Gradually experiment with one design after another, until you arrive at one that seems to fill the bill, and is aesthetically satisfying as well.

Here is a tentative design that could be taken as basic or suggestive:

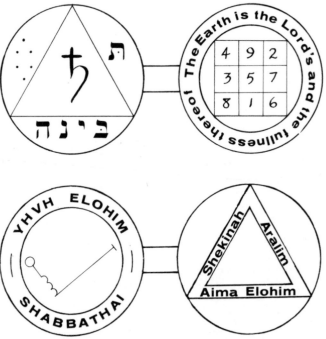

This incorporates most of the important symbols pertaining to Saturn, in its higher spiritual aspects. The concentrated effort to draw or paint this talisman would in itself go far towards correcting the flightiness and the scattering of mental energies which seems so often to accompany the Airy signs.

Meditation on the almost infinite meanings of these Saturn symbols should also help to implant in the depths of the psyche the spiritual essence required. Some form of ritual consecration should be attempted, after which the talisman, wrapped in an indigo silk pocket, should be carried on the person all the time.

The Seven Ancient Planets

The student should also seriously consider the advisability of making a talisman for each one of the seven ancient planets, and thus a different one for use every day of the week. In this manner, the daily use of the appropriate talisman may help rectify some of the astrological imbalances in his horoscope and in his personality make-up.

This idea is not necessarily new or revolutionary. It has been suggested before in a somewhat different area. Students of alchemy, familiar with what is called the Lesser Circulation, are taught that certain herbs are attributed to the influence of certain planets.

Such herbs can be prepared alchemically (see *The Alchemist's Handbook*, Weiser, New York), and a different one be self-administered every day. In this way, the planetary influences of a high potency are organismally absorbed to produce subtle far-reaching effects: physically, mentally, and spiritually.

The planetary talismans – the appropriate one worn on the person daily – are calculated to induce the same results, with far less effort and bother in their preparation. The principles already described will cover their construction. These personally designed talismans are much to be preferred to those copied from this or any other text.

3.

Words of Power

In the Hermetic Order of the Golden Dawn, a most interesting anachronism was employed to serve as the basis for the construction of sigils. It related to the old symbol of a Rose upon a Cross – not necessarily a new symbol in itself. However, it is not any antecedently known type of Rose-Cross Symbol. It has no parallels in occult or symbolic history. The novelty consisted of drawing the twenty-two Hebrew letters in the petals of the Rose according to the archaic attributions of *The Sepher Yetzirah*.

They were placed in a certain order. The so-called twelve single letters, referred to the twelve signs of the Zodiac, were placed in the outermost circle of rose petals. Within this ring were the seven double letters attributed to the seven planets. Inside this second ring, was a third subdivision of large petals where were found the three mother letters so-called, referred to the three prime elements of fire, water and air.

This resulted in the development of a simple but ingenious schema from which could be drawn an entirely new set of sigils, vastly different from those originally derived from the traditional magical squares. This complete symbol of the Rose

The Golden Dawn Rose of Twenty-Two Petals

on the Cross may be seen in one of the volumes of *The Golden Dawn* (Llewellyn Publications, St Paul, 1969), though the Rose itself, which is the only part of the symbol that concerns us, is reproduced here. The student will find himself amply repaid by experimenting with the drawing of sigils of every conceivable type of name on this Rose of twenty-two petals. He may find such sigils of more practical value than those made from the traditional Kameas.

Words and Versicles

On the various talismans that the student may perceive in the books referred to in the Bibliography, he will find various words and versicles inscribed in the circular margins on the periphery of the talisman. These versicles or words are also traditional. The words were, as a rule, biblical names of God, together with the names of angels, spirits and intelligences. Elaborate tables of these hierarchies have come down to us from the sources already mentioned. There follows such a Table of Names.

Element	Divine Names	Archangel & Enochian King	Angel	Ruler	King
Earth — Gnomes	Adonai ha-Aretz EMOR DIAL HECTEGA	Auriel IC ZOD HEH CHAL	Phorlach	Kerub	Ghob
Air — Sylphs	Shaddai El Chai ORO IBAH AOZPI	Raphael BATAIVAH	Chassan	Ariel	Paralda
Water — Undines	Elohim Tzabaoth EMPEH ARSL GAIOL	Gabriel RA AGIO-SEL	Taliahad	Tharsis	Nichsa
Fire — Salamanders	YHVH Tzabaoth OIP TEAA PEDOCE	Michael EDL-PERNAA	Aral	Seraph	Djin
Akasa — Spirit (Ether)	Eheieh and Agla	EXARP HCOMA NANTA BITOM	ELEXARPEH Yeheshuah COMANANU and TABITOM Yehovashah		

Table of Hierarchical Names

Scriptural Authorization

Moreover, phrases and sentences were extrapolated from both Old and New Testaments to provide authorization and power. It was not considered worth-while making a talisman unless it incorporated scriptural authorization of one kind or another. There was always some verse or reference to be found which could sanctify the use to which this particular talisman was about to be put.

Involved here is an archaic principle called commemoration. Its theory is simply that in the past God came to the aid of so-and-so, and performed such-and-such a feat for this person. An allusion to this event is required in the versicles used, as though to re-affirm the suggestion that such a divine feat may be repeated here and now, for me, by the same God who had previously done similar things.

For example, if I were an electrical engineer, under contract to build a new power station to provide light and power for a new village to be erected adjacent to an atomic installation, and needed inspiration to deal adequately with this project, I might construct a Solar talisman.

Since the structure would provide light, the talismanic ruler could well be the source of light and life to the earth, the Sun. An appropriate biblical verse for inscription around the outer margin of one side of the talisman could be: 'And God said, Let there be light. And there was light!'

The literary recording in the Bible of this prehistoric event provides justification and hope that an event modelled on the pattern of this earlier one may well be repeated, on request, as it were. An infinite variety of changes may be rung on this simple theme. But this provides the basic idea involved. Of course one has to be familiar with the books of the Bible to know where to look for the right phrase.

Classical Inscriptions

Traditionally also, the verse was written in Hebrew letters. Since, however, few students could letter Hebrew legibly and artistically, resulting in the occurrence of many stupid misprints or inartistic transcriptions, thus rendering null and void the intrinsic meaning of the biblical verses, some innovators came to use Latin.

There was somewhat less chance of miscopying in Latin: though this was found, even so, not to be altogether true. But there it was – Hebrew, Latin, and sometimes Greek were the classical languages used in writing inscriptions around the margin of the talismans, as may be seen by consulting *The Greater Key of King Solomon*.

The principles involved are still valid. For many years, when experimenting with talismans, I followed the ancient rules. And I must admit that when a little ingenuity and artistic inventiveness were employed, the results turned out to be very beautiful and striking, and certainly most effective. The student can be honestly counselled to follow the classical rule if he finds himself drawn in that direction, as I have been in the distant past.

4.

Talismans of the Five Elements

In this manual I would like to adapt these classical or ancient principles to a somewhat simpler and perhaps more modern style. The fundamental rules are still traditional and classical of course, but the method of application may be found more direct, and less arduous and obscure.

For example, I suggest that the selected verses from the Bible may be copied on to the talisman in English, without recourse to Hebrew or Latin or Greek if the reader is unfamiliar with these tongues. The only requirement is that he copy artistically. That is to say, the English lettering should be clear, as beautiful as he can possibly make it, and relevant to the subject held in mind.

A Wide Choice

Furthermore, I see no reason why the student should be confined to the Bible or any other single book for his authority in the projects involved.

The day has long since passed when the average intelligent person knew no other sacred scriptures than those of his own family, country and religion. If he knows the Koran, the

Bhagavad Gita, the Book of Mormon, or even Kahlil Gibran's exquisite masterpiece *The Prophet*, or keenly appreciates some lines from Shakespeare, Dante Gabriel Rossetti, or perhaps Charles Swinburne, there is no conceivable reason why these should not be used instead of some other.

The sole requirement is that the student should be *emotionally moved by* or involved in the quotation employed. In the last resort, let me assert here that rituals and talismans and all ceremonial magic become effective not only because of the employment of the trained will and imagination, but primarily by virtue of the affective arousal of which he is capable. Enthusiasm or a divine frenzy is the primary productive factor.

The Five Ancient Elements

Moreover, in place of the traditional seven planets, let me suggest a far simpler classification: that of the five ancient elements – Earth, Air, Water, Fire and Ether, the Quintessence. And going further, I believe we can find in the Golden Dawn attributions to these five elements a broad base of meaning into which most projects may be classified. Their divinatory meanings as given in the section on Tarot provide us with the major materials we need.

For example, the following may be used as our foundation:

Earth: Business, money, employment, practical affairs, etc.
Air: Health, sickness, disputations, trouble, etc.
Water: Pleasure, marriage, fertility, happiness, parties, etc.
Fire: Power, dominion, authority, prestige, etc.
Ether: All matters spiritual, howsoever they are interpreted.

The symbols for these five elements may be of several kinds, though for the purpose of this interpretation, I have conveniently selected the Tattvic system of the East, as follows:

Earth: Prithivi, a yellow square. *Heh* (final) of Tetragrammaton.
Air: Vayu, a blue circle. *Vav* of Tetragrammaton.
Water: Apas, a silver crescent. *Heh* of Tetragrammaton.
Fire: Tejas, a red triangle. *Yod* of Tetragrammaton.
Ether (Spirit): *Akasa*, a black egg. *Shin* of Pentagrammaton.

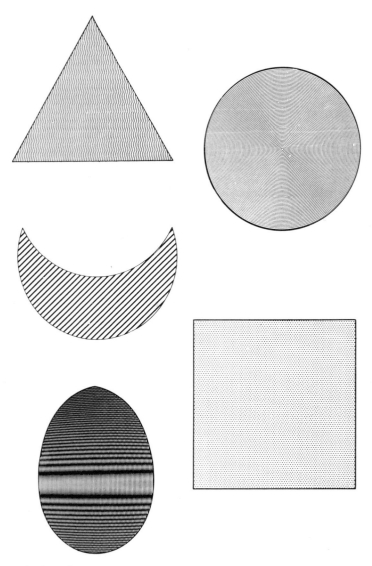

Artistic Schema

This immediately provides an artistic schema for the creation
of talismans. A fire talisman could be constructed out of bright
red-coloured papers, similar to the Japanese origama, in the
form of an upright triangle. Appropriate inscriptions,

writings, and sigils could be written on it in green ink or paint. The result would be a flashing talisman, that is, the use of complementary colours would result in ocular flashings, as a little experimental work will prove.

An earth talisman could be made out of a yellow square of coloured paper, with the writing in purple or mauve, depending on the intensity and hue of the yellow.

Liberties or artistic licence can be taken with the shapes, depending on the number and size of sigils or barbarous words of power or phrases that one wishes to use.

For example, a double triangle for *Tejas* could be cut with a connecting slip or tab of red paper. Opened out, it would yield four triangular sides, thus providing more space on which to write. When finished, it could be folded together on the tab as follows:

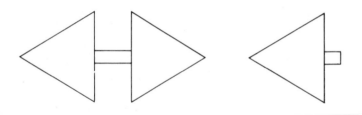

Once the student becomes familiar with the schema by working at it, and reflecting on it for a while, he will gain an enormous amount of data to be used in this way. There are many changes to be rung on this simple schema.

Tarot Symbols
Some of the symbols on the Tarot cards could be reproduced to great advantage on the talismans, if the student wishes. For instance, if he were making a talisman to produce pleasure and joy, the Ace of Cups in any of the conventional packs is a beautiful symbol to be copied in ink or painted on to the silver crescent of Apas.

For spiritual help in the hour of trouble, the sword and crown of the Ace of Swords – which literally means invoked strength – would be an ideal symbol to transpose on to the blue circle of Vayu. The need for change in an otherwise dull poverty-stricken existence could well be represented by the Two of Pentacles in the Golden Dawn suit.

Incidentally, there is no need to be a slavish imitator when making talismans. Even though the symbol for Earth is the yellow square, the student could still make a conventional circular talisman on which to draw Prithivi.

In the case of the silver half-circle or crescent of Apas, the circular talisman could still be made, and then draw the cresecent on it with such other symbols as he deems appropriate. This discussion is purely arbitrary, and is intended simply to stimulate the ingenium or latent creativity of the student.

The alchemical symbols for the elements could be studied merely to provide additional symbols to use when opportunity or necessity warrants:

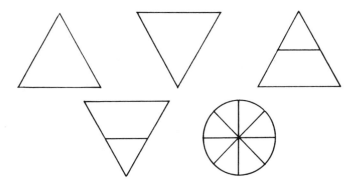

Tradition has attributed a vast series of hierarchical names to each of these five elements, extrapolated from several sources, all of which will be found useful both in creating the talisman properly, as well as in ceremonially 'charging' it.

This table (see Chapter Three), provides most of the basic information relative to the elemental hierarchies that is needed in order to draw, paint, or otherwise create any talisman in terms of the five elements, as already described. It also contributes the necessary data for use in any ceremonial ritual undertaken to consecrate the resultant talisman.

Building an Angelic Name

There is one more set of symbols that should be mentioned. It is an angelic name built up from the zodiacal triplicities, and is described by Mathers in a Golden Dawn paper in these words:

> Having made a magical talisman, you should use some form of charging and consecrating it, which is suitable to the operation. There are certain traditional words and letters which are to be invoked in the charging of a Tablet, the letters governing the Sign under which the operation falls, together with the Planet associated therewith (if a planetary talisman). Thus in Elemental operations, you should take the Letters of the appropriate zodiacal triplicity, adding AL thereto, thus forming an Angelic Name which is the expression of the force. Hebrew Names as a rule represent the operation of certain general forces, while the names on the Enochian or Angelical Tablets represent a species of more particular ideas. Both classes of names should be used in these operations.

I illustrate his idea as follows:

Fire Triplicity:	Air Triplicity:	Water Triplicity:	Earth Triplicity:
Aries *Heh*	Gemini *Zayin*	Cancer *Cheth*	Taurus *Vav*
Leo *Teth*	Libra *Lamed*	Scorpio *Nun*	Virgo *Yod*
Sagittarius *Samech*	Aquarius *Tzaddi*	Pisces *Qoph*	Capricorn *Ayin*
+ AL = *Hitsael*	+ AL = *Zaltzel*	+ AL = *Chankel*	+ AL = *Vioel*

These names should either be incorporated into the talisman itself, or sigils based upon them should be traced, during a ceremony, over the talisman, as though standing upon it, while the angelic Name is vibrated strongly and often.

5.

A Practical Example

The clarification of all the above theoretical points can best be achieved by means of a practical example.

Let us assume that in the critical analysis of my character-structure, I find that I am on the whole sombre, serious and reserved, and that I have but little capacity for pleasure. In other words I am not capable of getting much fun out of life. Having arrived at this conclusion, magical study informs me that these character defects can best be remedied by the invocation of the higher powers of the element of Water, to which joy and happiness are attributed.

The effect of such invocation can best be prolonged or perpetuated by making a talisman dedicated to Water. By making it carefully and artistically, by charging it in due ceremonial form, and wearing it on my person at all times, the intention is that the constant sensory stimulus it affords may evoke out of the unconscious depths of my psyche the latent potencies of the pleasure-principle which have been suppressed by virtue of early puritanical training. We could also say that it will act as a constant reminder of the presence and power of God.

Silver Paper

Water being the element required to remedy the character defect, I select a large piece of heavy silver paper on which to paint names and symbols in peach water-colours or poster paints. The size of the silver crescent, Apas, will be determined mostly by convenience, first in working with it on the drawing board, and secondly as to whether it will fit into my wallet.

A four-inch diameter circular talisman is perhaps the most convenient. In order to have as many sides as possible on which to draw as large a variety of symbols as I possibly can, it is decided to use a double sphere connected by a tab, thus:

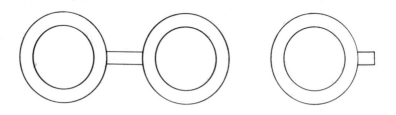

1. Open   2. Folded

Ace of Cups

On one of the sides, it seems that a peculiarly appropriate symbol would be the Ace of Cups from, let us say, the Waite or Golden Dawn pack of the Tarot cards, using as many of the colours on my talisman as are found on the card. It also sets the tone for the entire project, its formal meaning and description being given in the Golden Dawn documents as a radiant white Angelic hand issuing from clouds and supporting a cup.

From the cup rises a fountain of clear, glistening water. Spray falls on all sides into clear calm water below, in which grow Lotus and water lilies. The great letter *Heh* of the Supernal Mother is traced in the spray of the fountain, symbolizing fertility, productiveness, beauty, pleasure, happiness, etc.

Basic Intention

The next step is to assemble the divine names pertaining to this element, and a sentence or so which will express and formalize my basic intention.

Instead of selecting a verse from the Bible as previously might have been the case, I am reminded of two separate verses which would be considered appropriate. The first one is adapted from one of the Golden Dawn rituals reading: 'Blessed be Thou, Father of the undying, for Thy glory flows out rejoicing, even to the ends of the earth!' The second is from Crowley's *Book of the Law*: 'But ecstasy be thine and joy of earth.'

Both verses are excellent. After due reflection, however, I decide in favour of that from *The Book of the Law*, as being more apt to my purpose. So then, with great and loving care, using a fine brush or a special lettering pen, I print the 'ecstasy' versicle on the second side of the talisman in such a way as to create for me the most pleasing design or emotional effect.

Enochian Divine Names

On side three, the appropriate Enochian divine names are inscribed around the circumference. 'The Three most secret Holy Names of God' as the rituals describe them, **EMPEH ARSL GAIOL,** are printed on the upper portion of the circumference, while the divine King's name (based on the central whorl) is printed below – **RA AGIOSEL**. They could have been lettered in the Angelic tongue, but I have decided to do this in English script in order to complete my total break with tradition.

In the centre, the appropriate Hebrew God-name for the element is written in. Instead of using classical Hebrew script, I decide once more to use capital Romans which create an equally good effect, one in line with my avowed intention of departing from blind tradition and innovating a more simple procedure. These names, **YHVH TZABAOTH**, I arrange on side one, around the cup design of the Tarot pack, instead of on side three as originally contemplated, as making a better design.

As explained before, the traditional sigil of the Archangel *Gabriel* drawn from the magical square as given in Barret's

Magus could have been used. Instead, however, on side three I propose to trace the sigil on the Golden Dawn Rose.

The name *Gabriel* should then be converted into Hebrew letters, only for the purpose of making a tracing of its letters on the accompanying Rose. Volume I of *The Golden Dawn* gives this name and many other hierarchical ones in Hebrew, so that there should be no problem in making the sigil. The tracing then will look like this:

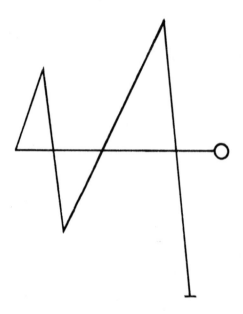

Merely for convenience sake, start the first letter G with a small circle, ending the last letter L with a short dash.

This sigil should then be most carefully drawn in the centre of the circle. There are no established rules as to how this should be done. The student's own sense of design or his 'right ingenium' is the only factor to be considered.

For the centre of the fourth side, my decision is to make a large sigil of the elemental King whose name is Taliahad. This name is converted into Hebrew, which again will be found in Volume I of *The Golden Dawn*, so there is no problem here. Its tracing on the Rose is thus:

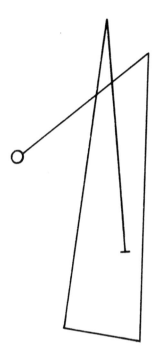

Though it is not absolutely essential, I propose to use one last set of symbols – the geomantic symbols and the emblems derived from them. There are three symbols attributed to the Watery triplicity, but since Rubeus for Scorpio is patently an evil sign, it is best omitted, leaving only Populus for Cancer and Laetitia for Pisces.

Populus is drawn thus:
And from it several little
emblematic designs may be
drawn with ease.

```
x   x
x   x
x   x
x   x
```

Laetitia is thus:
And its emblems may be
drawn so:

These symbols therefore may be placed around the circumference of the circle, together with the traditional symbol of Water, the inverted Triangle. We would also include what the Golden Dawn called the Kerub of Water, the Eagle's Head, representing the sublimation of the intrinsic energy of Scorpio as the active power of God operating through the element water. Thus:

All of these symbols, including the silver crescent of Apas, should be placed on side four of the talisman.

Rough Drafts

Incidentally, I suggest several rough drafts should be attempted first, until one is gradually evolved that is entirely pleasing to the student. Then it should be painstakingly copied on to the final parchment, vellum, or coloured paper which will be the finished talisman.

Make it a cardinal rule *never* to leave the rough drafts of any kind of magical design lying around carelessly. Once the student has finished with them, they should be meticulously destroyed and burned. After all, they are symbols of divinity and should be respected as such. The final and finished copy, before being wrapped in a pocket of silk, should look something like this:

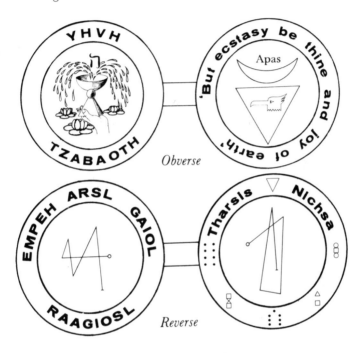

Obverse

Reverse

6.

How to Charge the Talisman

This completes the first part of the operation. I would say that merely having completed the mechanical drawing of the talisman, in the best manner possible and with concentration, would invest it with a good deal of force. How much energy is involved depends entirely on the skill and development of the student. If he has the 'know-how' the talisman can be charged or consecrated all the way through the process of drawing it.

In that case, carrying the talisman on one's person would, by its constant presence and suggestion, go far toward gradually eliciting the desired response. If however the student is just beginning his studies in this area, not much of a magical charge will be contributed to the talisman while making it. In that case, the ancient tradition demands a further process.

Dead Material
The magical position is that, under these circumstances, the talisman itself is nothing but dead and inert material. It may well be compared with the candidate for initiation. Of himself, he can do nothing. He has tried to lift himself up by his own

bootstraps, but to no avail. Now the process of initiation, activated by skilled practitioners of the art of initiation, takes over with a view to opening the candidate to higher forces.

Much the same viewpoint is adopted relative to the talisman. It requires to be activated by the forces of higher planes. As Crowley once put it extremely well:

> It will be seen that the effect of this whole ceremony is to endow a thing inert and impotent with balanced motion in a given direction ... It is the formula of the Neophyte Ceremony of the G.D. It should be employed in the consecration of the actual weapons used by the magician, and may also be used as the first formula of initiation.

There are at least two distinct approaches relative to this matter of consecrating or charging the talisman with a specific type of energy. The first method is predicated upon a species of meditation, the second is a ceremonial magical consecration. We will consider each briefly in turn.

The Middle Pillar

It would be infinitely useful if the student of this manual were familiar with an earlier essay of mine based on some elementary Golden Dawn formulae. It is called 'The Art of True Healing' (in *Foundations of Practical Magic*, Aquarian Press, 1979), and describes a process based on the Qabalistic Tree of Life called The Middle Pillar, which can readily be adapted to the task of charging the talisman thus prepared.

The opening phases of this process consist in highly charging the aura or sphere of sensation of the student with energy. It is followed by changing the colour of the electromagnetic field, by an effort of imagination, to that of the element being considered.

In this case, the element is Water and, in that particular system, is coloured blue, When the field is charged with this blue colour, the appropriate names on the talisman itself are frequently vibrated, and if the talisman is held in the hand it becomes charged inductively by a strong current of energy. When completed, it should be wrapped in a piece of clean linen or coloured silk, preferably made in the form of a pocket into which it may be slipped.

Golden Dawn Consecration

The second method has been briefly described in Volume IV of *The Golden Dawn*. The student who has gone thus far, and has to some extent studied the technical procedures once used in this magical Order, should have no difficulty understanding or applying the following instruction.

After preparing the room in the way laid down for the consecration of lesser magical implements, supposing this to be an Elemental Talisman, first formulate towards the four Quarters the Supreme Ritual of the Pentagram as taught. Then invoke the Divine Names turning towards the quarter of the Element.

Let the Adeptus then, being seated or standing before the Tablet, and looking in the requisite direction of the force which he wishes to invoke, take several deep inspirations, close the eyes, and holding the breath, mentally pronounce the letters of the Forces invoked. Let this be done several times, as if you breathed upon the Tablet pronouncing them in the vibratory manner. Then, rising, make the sign of the Rose and Cross over the Tablet, and repeating the requisite formula, first describe around the Talisman a circle, with the appropriate magical implement, and then make the invoking Pentagrams five times over it, as if the Pentagrams stood upright upon it, repeating the letters of the Triplicity involved with AL added. Then solemnly read any invocation required, making the proper sigils from the Rose as you pronounce the Names.

The first operation is to initiate a whirl from yourself. The second, to attract the Force in the atmosphere into the vortex you have formed.

Then read the Elemental Prayer as in the Rituals, and close with the Signs of the Circle and the Cross (that is the Rose-Cross) after performing the necessary Banishing.

'Be careful, however, not to banish over the newly consecrated Talisman, as that would simply decharge it again and render it useless. Before Banishing, you should wrap the charged Talisman in clean white silk or linen.

7.

Examples of Sigils

Venus is attributed to the Sephirah Netzach, which is numbered 7 on the Tree of Life. Thus its Kamea is a large square of 49 smaller squares and numbers. Notice that the diagonal from the upper left corner to the lower right hand corner includes the numbers from 22–28. The other diagonal from the upper right to lower left hand corner proceeds from the number 4 at intervals of 7, to 46. (*See* Kamea of Venus, *page 18*).

The sigil Hagiel should have a much shorter bar on the left side, since it runs from 1 to 3 on the Kamea.

The planet Sun is attributed to Tiphareth, which is the 6th Sephirah. Thus its number is 6, and the Kamea has 36 squares.

The Seal quite evidently connects up every square on the Kamea in its specific design.

The other two Sigils are relatively simple and should present no problems in tracing.

The Kamea of Mars, comprising 25 squares and numbers, is the basis of this Seal and these Sigils. Be patient and take your time in working out how these symbols are formed. The principle follows through on all of them.

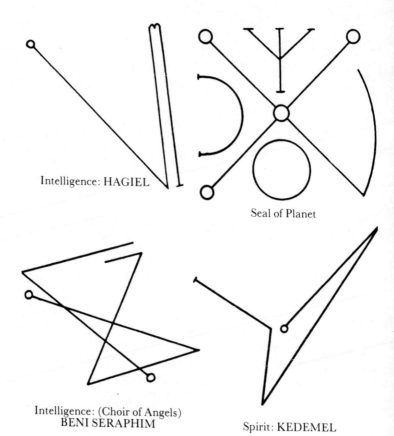

Intelligence: HAGIEL

Seal of Planet

Intelligence: (Choir of Angels)
BENI SERAPHIM

Spirit: KEDEMEL

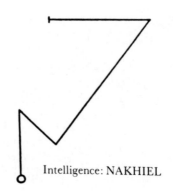

Intelligence: NAKHIEL

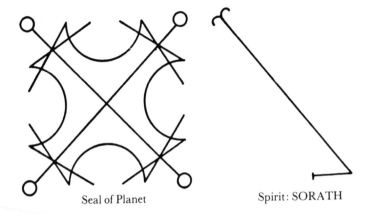

Seal of Planet

Spirit: SORATH

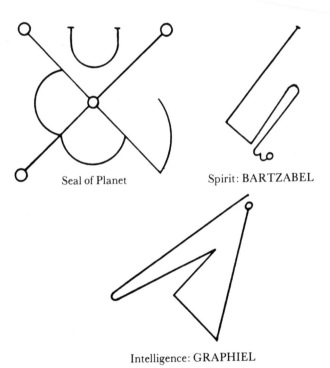

Seal of Planet

Spirit: BARTZABEL

Intelligence: GRAPHIEL

The Seal of the Planet Saturn is undoubtedly the simplest of the seals to understand. The Kamea has nine squares, and of course numbers. Each number is touched by the lines of the Seal. There should be no difficulty working this out. If the student takes time to try to understand this Seal and the Sigils relating to it, the other more complex Seals and Sigils will not prove to be insuperable problems.

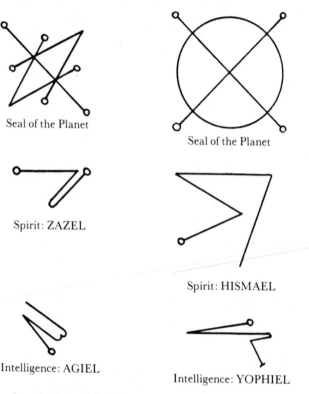

Seal of the Planet

Seal of the Planet

Spirit: ZAZEL

Spirit: HISMAEL

Intelligence: AGIEL

Intelligence: YOPHIEL

What has been said of Saturn is also true of Jupiter, of which this is the Seal.

The patterns become slightly more complex with the addition or progression of each number. But if the basic theory is adhered to, the student will be able to follow development of the various symbols – from the Seal to the different Sigils.

The Mercury Square or Kameas is a figure of 64 squares. The figures are somewhat more difficult to trace out. This would be in keeping with the traditional notion of Mercury being the Trickster – a deceiver and a liar.

The only figure about which I have experienced some problems as I experiment with it now – after the lapse of forty or more years when I worked these out in great detail – is the Sigil of Tiriel. I suspect that the drawing is simply reversed. Reverse it, and it fits on to the Kamea quite well.

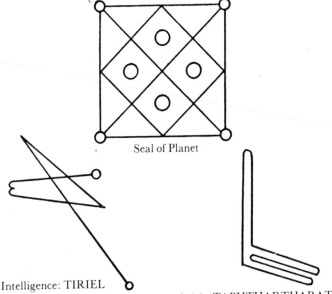

Seal of Planet

Intelligence: TIRIEL

Spirit: TAPHTHARTHARATH

The Seal is usually a design so arranged that every number on the square will be touched and so included within the design. It follows of course that any number of designs could be made that would fulfil this requirement. This is the one that has come down, hallowed as it were, from tradition.

The Sigils are signatures of beings related to that planet. The original Hebrew is translated into the appropriate numbers which are then traced out on the square.

These Sigils relating to the Moon appear to be more complex than those of the other planets. Basically this is

because the Moon is attributed to the 9th Sephirah, Yesod.
Therefore the Kamea has 81 squares on which the long
Angelic names are traced.

Spirit: CHASHMODAI

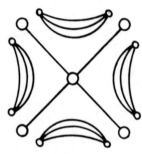

Seal of Planet

Spirit of the Spirits of the Moon:
SHAD BARSCHEMOTH HA-
SCHARTATHAN

Intelligence of the Intelligences of the Moon: MALCAH
BETARSHISIM VE-AD RUACHOTH HA-SCHECHALIM

Appendixes

This Tree of Life is a fairly complex glyph, because it incorporates so many different features. Includes the Lightning Flash, tracing the descent of the divine light in creation – and of course in illumination. It also includes the Serpent of Wisdom, relating to the Way of Return. And on each Sephirah is given the divine Name, Archangelic Name and the Choir of Angels – thus relating to three of the Four Qabalistic Worlds.

The connecting links between each Sephirah are the Paths, on which are simply the letter of the Alphabet, the number of the Path, and by implication – though not specifically stated – the corresponding Tarot card.

The whole philosophy of the Qabalah is summed up in this symbol. It takes a lifetime fully to appreciate its complexity and its meaning.

The Tree of Life

THE HEBREW ALPHABET

Letter	Power	Value	Final	Name	Meaning
א	A	1		Aleph	Ox
ב	B, V	2		Beth	House
ג	G, Gh	3		Gimel	Camel
ד	D, Dh	4		Daleth	Door
ה	H	5		He	Window
ו	O,U,V	6		Vau	Pin or Hook
ז	Z	7		Zayin	Sword or Armour
ח	Ch	8		Cheth	Fence, Enclosure
ט	T	9		Teth	Snake
י	I, Y	10		Yod	Hand
כ	K, Kh	20,500	ך	Kaph	Fist
ל	L	30		Lamed	Ox Goad
מ	M	40,600	ם	Mem	Water
נ	N	50,700	ן	Nun	Fish
ס	S	60		Samekh	Prop
ע	Aa,Ngh	70		Ayin	Eye
פ	P, Ph	80,800	ף	Pe	Mouth
צ	Tz	90,900	ץ	Tzaddi	Fish-hook
ק	Q	100		Qoph	Ear. Back of Head
ר	R	200		Resh	Head
ש	S, Sh	300		Shin	Tooth
ת	T, Th	400		Tau	Cross

ATTRIBUTION OF THE TAROT TRUMPS

Path	No.	Tarot Trump	Letter	Symbol
11	0	The Foolish Man	א	🜁
12	1	The Juggler	ב	☿
13	2	The High Priestess	ג	☽
14	3	The Empress	ד	♀
15	4	The Emperor	ה	♈
16	5	The Hierophant	ו	♉
17	6	The Lovers	ז	♊
18	7	The Chariot	ח	♋
19	8	Strength	ט	♌
20	9	The Hermit (Prudence)	י	♍
21	10	The Wheel of Fortune	כ	♃
22	11	Justice	ל	♎
23	12	The Hanged Man	מ	🜄
24	13	Death	נ	♏
25	14	Temperance	ס	♐
26	15	The Devil	ע	♑
27	16	Tower Struck by Lightning	פ	♂
28	17	The Star	צ	♒
29	18	The Moon	ק	♓
30	19	The Sun	ר	☉
31	20	Last Judgment	ש	🜂
32	21	The Universe	ת	♄

Bibliography

Barrett, Francis, *The Magus* Thorsons Publishers Limited, England 1977.
Crowley, Aleister, *Magick* Castle Books, New York.
Gray, William G., *Ladder of Lights* Helios, England 1968.
Mathers, S.L. McGregor (trans.), *The Greater Key of Solomon*.
—, Aleister Crowley (ed.), *Lesser Key of King Solomon (The Goetia)*.
Raphael, *Book of Talismans*.
Regardie, Israel, *A Garden of Pomegranates* Llewellyn Publications, St Paul 1970.
—, *The Golden Dawn* Llewellyn Publications, St Paul 1969.
—, *The Tree of Life* Samuel Weiser Inc., New York 1969.
Waite, Arthur E., *The Book of Ceremonial Magic* University Books, New York.